IN SEARCH OF
THE MAIASAURS

IN SEARCH OF THE MAIASAURS

by

Dorothy Hinshaw Patent

BENCHMARK BOOKS

MARSHALL CAVENDISH
NEW YORK

Grateful acknowledgment is made to Dr. Kenneth Carpenter,
Chief Preparator and Dinosaur Paleontologist at the Denver Museum of
Natural History, Denver, Colorado.

Benchmark Books
Marshall Cavendish Corporation
99 White Plains Road
Tarrytown, New York 10591-9001

Library of Congress Cataloging-in-Publication Data
Patent, Dorothy Hinshaw.
In search of the maiasaurs / Dorothy Hinshaw Patent.
p.   cm. — (Frozen in time)
Includes bibliographical references and index.
Summary: Describes the discovery and study of fossil records revealing the herding and
nesting behavior of the dinosaur known as Maiasaura.
ISBN 0-7614-0787-1
1. Maiasaura—Montana—Juvenile literature. 2. Animals, Fossil—Montana—Juvenile
literature. 3. Paleontology—Juvenile literature. 4. Horner, John R. [1. Maiasaura. 2.
Dinosaurs. 3. Fossils. 4. Paleontology.] I. Title. II. Series; Patent, Dorothy Hinshaw.
Frozen in time.
QE862.065P38   1999   567'.914—DC21   97-46733   CIP   AC

Printed in Hong Kong

3 5 6 4

Photo research by Linda Sykes Picture Research, Hilton Head, SC
Book design by Carol Matsuyama

Photo Credits
Front cover: courtesy of © Douglas Henderson; Title page: © Douglas Henderson from
Maia. A Dinosaur Grows Up by John Horner & James Gormon, published by the Museum
of the Rockies; pages 7, 8–9, 11, 14–15, 32–33, 36, 41, 44, 46: Bruce Selyem © Museum
of the Rockies; page 10: Terry Panasuk © Museum of the Rockies; page 12–13:
© John Kaprielian/Photo Researchers, Inc.; page 18–19: Douglas Henderson © Museum of
the Rockies; pages 20, 21, 38–39, 51 (top): Natural History Museum, London; pages 22–23,
28–29: © Douglas Henderson from *Living With Dinosaurs* by Patricia Lauber, published by
Bradbury Press; page 25: Natural History Museum/Orbis; page 26: © Douglas Henderson;
page 27: National Geographic Image Collection; page 30–31: Peabody Museum of Natural
History; page 35: © 1996 Hans Larsson/Matrix; page 43: James L. Amos/Photo Researchers;
page 45: Museum of the Rockies; page 48–49: J. Sibbick/Natural History Museum; page 51
(bottom): Louis Psihoyos/Matrix; page 52: © 1988 Donna Braginetz

Contents

Introduction

THE MYSTERY OF THE GIANT BONE BED

I've always been fascinated by dinosaurs, and for years, I've wanted to write about these amazing and mysterious creatures of the past. But finding something new and different to say about dinosaurs isn't easy. My opportunity came purely by chance.

A small display in the Museum of the Rockies in Bozeman, Montana, caught my eye. It was entitled "A Gigantic Accumulation of Maiasaur Bones" and included a small sample from the largest concentration of dinosaur bones found anywhere in the world. It was part of a bone bed almost 2 square miles (5.2 square kilometers) in area. With a density of thirty bones per square yard, it is the graveyard for thousands of dinosaurs, almost all of a single species, or kind.

I saw immediately that the mystery of this giant bone bed provided a perfect way to explain the work of paleontologists—scientists who study fossils from ancient times to learn about the living things of the past. The bone bed could also show how we now think dinosaurs lived in their environment millions of years ago. For me, the most exciting thing about dinosaurs is bringing them to life, imagining how they might have behaved and comparing them to the animals that live today. Even though dinosaurs have been extinct for 65 million years and more, reconstructing how they probably lived is sometimes possible. When scientists find enough material, they can use the universal principles of biology, which apply as much to ancient environments as to today's, to reveal the secrets of the past.

Here is one small part of the giant maiasaur bone bed found in Montana.

1
DISCOVERY OF A DINOSAUR HERD

The enormous bone bed wasn't found in one exciting moment of discovery. Like most work in the field of paleontology, it occurred over a period of years, through hard work and great patience.

In 1979, Marion and John Brandvold, who owned a rock shop in northwestern Montana, were digging on a nearby ranch. They were hoping to find a big dinosaur skeleton that they could reconstruct for display at their shop. Paleontologist Jack Horner and his colleagues were working in the same area. The Brandvolds would need help digging up and moving the

◄ *The area in northwestern Montana where the bone bed was found* skeleton if they were lucky enough to find one. So, in exchange for help from Horner's group, they agreed to map the site of their find and catalog the bones for the scientists.

John and Marion Brandvold, who first found the bones of baby maiasaurs

Paleontologists do their field-work from late spring to early fall. When Horner returned for the 1980 field season, he looked over the Brandvolds' material. Unfortunately for them, the many bones at their site could not be assembled into the skeleton of one animal. Instead, they were a jumbled mixture of mostly broken bones, from a number of animals. While the Brandvolds were disappointed, Horner was interested. He could tell that the bones came from at least five dinosaurs, all of the same species. Three of them were young individuals, and the other two were adults. Maybe this was a dinosaur family, he thought, all killed at the same place and time.

Then, in 1981, Horner's eight-year-old son, Jason, found a batch of big bones like those found earlier at the Brandvold site. Jason's site was about an eighth of a mile (two-tenths of a kilometer) away, in the same layer of rock. When the scientists checked, they found that the bone deposit extended all the way between the two sites. These weren't the remains of just one family of dinosaurs.

That same year, one of Horner's workers found still more bones of the same type right in their camp, under the place he tried to set up his tent. He couldn't get comfortable, because the dinosaur bones kept poking him in the back. When the group decided to investigate this site, they ended up digging a big pit in the middle of the camp. Over the years, the pit yielded 4,500 bone pieces. They were of the same species that were found at the other two sites. The scientists dubbed this site Camposaur, since it was in the middle of their camp.

Not far from Camposaur, a group of visiting children were allowed to help dig for dinosaur fossils. Because there were so many bones at this site, and because they were so similar to those in Camposaur, Horner felt that losing a few specimens to amateur errors would not be a problem. The Children's site and Camposaur were clearly parts of the same bone deposit. Similarly, the Brandvold site and Jason's (which he named Nose Cone because the rock looked like the tip of a rocket) were part of one deposit. But were both deposits connected so that they formed a really enormous dinosaur bone bed?

A boy helps uncover fossils at the Children's site.

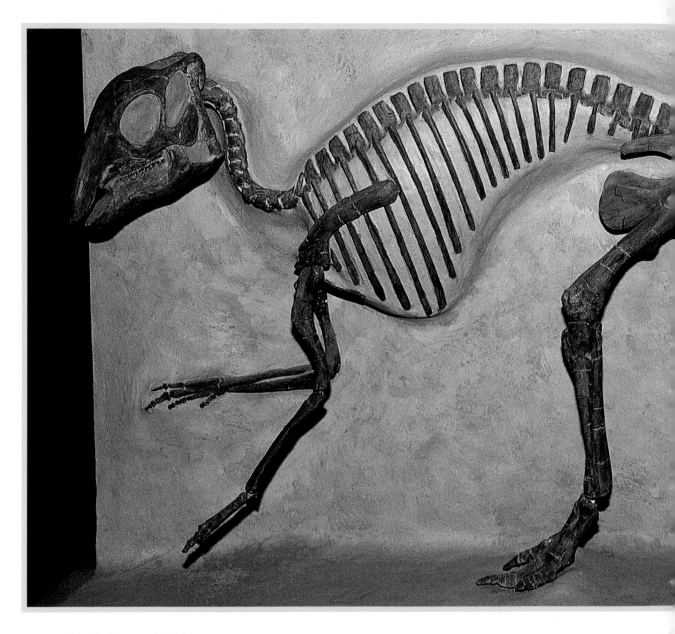

The skeleton of Maiasaura

One day in 1981, Horner sat on a hill overlooking the two areas. He thought about the fact that the same kinds of black, broken-up bones were found in each. By then, he had confirmed that the bones all belonged to a newly discovered species of dinosaur, which he had recently identified, named *Maiasaura peeblesorum*. He decided to check and see if this really was one big maiasaur graveyard.

Horner measured the vertical (up-and-down) distance in both

areas to another layer of fossil-containing rock. The bone bed in the Brandvold/Nose Cone area and in the Camposaur/Children's site were the same vertical distance from the other layer, indicating that all four sites were probably part of the same bone deposit. Perhaps the paleontologists had, indeed, found a place where thousands of dinosaurs had all died at the same time, but they needed more evidence to be sure.

2

THE FIND

The giant bone bed was a fascinating find. But by 1984, after several years of study, the paleontologists felt that it would soon be time to move on to new areas. The 1984 field season—from June to September—would be their last at this site. Near the end of the season, Horner and one of his students, Will Gavin, took a walk near the Children's dig. Gavin had been studying the geology of the area and was showing Horner some of his interesting discoveries. Suddenly Gavin saw something no one had noticed before. About eighteen inches (forty-six centimeters) above the bone layer at the Children's site was a distinct layer of volcanic ash.

Part of the giant bone bed, these are blackened, fossilized bones of Maiasaura. ▶

Horner and Gavin realized immediately that if they found the ash layer the same distance above the other areas where the broken-up maiasaur bones lay, it would be certain evidence that they all represented the same bone deposit.

That's just what the men found—the ash lay the same distance above the bones at each of the four sites. It was also present at some additional sites nearby, including some quite far away. Now the scientists could be certain—here was a gigantic bed of fossilized bones, a quarter of a mile (four-tenths of a kilometer) long and a mile and a quarter (two kilometers) wide. If the bones were equally distributed throughout the area, they represented the death of at least ten thousand maiasaurs, an enormous thundering herd before disaster struck.

Elements of the Mystery

Here was a unique find. Up to that time, in 1984, no deposit of so many specimens of just one kind of dinosaur had ever been found. But how had the animals died? How had the bones come to lie in one place?

It seemed very doubtful that the dinosaurs had actually died where their fossilized bones now lay. In most of the deposit, there were almost no small bones, such as toes. If the animals had died there, all sizes of bones should have been present together. Instead, the smaller bones were concentrated at the eastern edge of the bone bed. Perhaps the dinosaurs had died and their bones had been washed together at the bend of an ancient river, as often happened. But bones carried by water would be left lying flat, and some of the bones in this collection had been standing upright. Maybe the animals were caught in a mudslide. That would explain why some bones were standing up. But many of the bones had been badly damaged—split lengthwise or crushed. And almost all the bones were pointing in the same direction, lying with their ends pointing east and west. If the mudslide had caught the animals alive, the bones wouldn't have been separated from one another, and they couldn't have been split while still cushioned by layers of muscle and fat.

It seemed that the bone bed was the result of two separate disasters. The first killed the enormous dinosaur herd, whose bodies then rotted away from their bones. Later on, yet another disaster swept the bones away, taking apart the skeletons, breaking some of the bones, and depositing them at the giant bone bed.

The Killing Field

A graduate student named Jeff Hooker took on the task of trying to figure out what had happened to this huge dinosaur herd. Millions of years ago, Montana was alive with volcanoes that erupted frequently as the Rocky Mountains were building to the west of the area where the bone bed was found.

Volcanoes can kill plants and animals in a number of different ways. Lava flows roll across the land, burying everything in their path. Ash rains down, suffocating plants and animals alike. The heat from volcanic activity can melt ice and liquefy mud, breaking down the dams that hold in lakes and causing tremendous floods of mud and water. Volcanoes also release clouds of poisonous gas that can kill in an instant.

After studying the ancient bone bed, Jeff Hooker came to the conclusion that the maiasaurs were killed by the smoke, gas, and ash from a huge volcanic eruption. The maiasaurs weren't the only animals killed—everything for miles around probably succumbed to the disaster, since there is no sign that scavengers fed on the carcasses. If they had, fossils of some of the scavengers' teeth probably would have been mixed in with the maiasaur bones.

Instead, the carcasses probably just lay there, baking in the sun, meat rotting away until only the bones remained. The second disaster, probably a mudflow, occurred long after the death of the dinosaurs. When it came, it swept away everything in its path and spread the bones out over the landscape, depositing the heavier leg and body bones first, at the western end of the bone bed, and the lighter bones of the feet and pieces of the skulls last, at the eastern end.

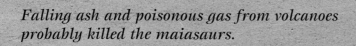

Falling ash and poisonous gas from volcanoes probably killed the maiasaurs.

How Fossils Form

The word *fossil* comes from Latin and simply means "something dug up." But a fossil is much more than that. It's a trace of life from ancient times that has come down to us, preserved, so we can puzzle over it and appreciate the tremendous amount of time that life existed on earth before we came into being.

Basically, a fossil consists of either the remains of a once living thing preserved close to its original shape or some product of an ancient organism, such as a footprint, tunnel, or fecal material. The most familiar fossils are of bones, shells, or the impression of plant parts such as leaves.

The process of forming fossils, called fossilization, usually begins when a dead plant or animal gets buried by sand or mud before the wood in the plant or bone in the animal decays. Over time, minerals in the

After this fish was buried, minerals replaced some of the material in its bones. Even the outline of the fish has been preserved in the fossil.

water gradually replace some of the organic matter in the wood or bone. This strengthens the developing fossil so that the layers of mud or sand that build up over it don't crush it. As the years go by, more and more layers are deposited on top of the fossil. The pressure from the weight of the layers compacts the mud or sand and turns it into stone. Soft-bodied creatures, such as jellyfish, may also be fossilized as an impression between layers of fine mud that become rock such as shale.

Why are some areas rich with fossils while other places have none? It all depends on how the rocks in an area were formed. Fossils are found in what are called sedimentary rocks, which form when layers of sand, volcanic ash, or mud are laid down and eventually harden into rock.

Most dinosaur fossils formed after the animals were buried during a flood or by a volcanic eruption. But many fossils formed at the bottoms of seas or lakes. If they had stayed there, we would never have found them. Over millions of years, however, the surface of the earth has changed. Movements of the earth's crust have thrust sea bottoms upward, sometimes even up to the tops of mountains.

This prehistoric fly was trapped in tree resin, which then hardened into amber. The amber has been polished to display the fly.

When fossil deposits are exposed to the air, they begin to erode. Wind, rain, frost, and running water wear away at the layers of rock. As they do so, the fossils hidden within are revealed. The material making up the fossil is different from the surrounding rock and wears away more slowly.

Paleontologists like Jack Horner sometimes find fossil traces and leave them until the following year to allow the weather to do some of the digging for them. Horner's group left one of the maiasaur nests they found for two years until erosion revealed its outline more clearly.

Some fossils are formed in other ways. Dinosaur eggs and nests found in Mongolia were preserved when blowing desert sands covered them. Amber, which forms by the hardening of sticky tree resin, often preserves the complete bodies of insects and spiders. Very rarely, paleontologists find the frozen carcasses of extinct animals such as mammoths or woolly rhinoceroses in the Arctic. Fossils of tracks left when animals walked across mud can be very helpful in figuring out how fast the animals may have walked and run.

3
DUCK-BILLED DINOSAURS

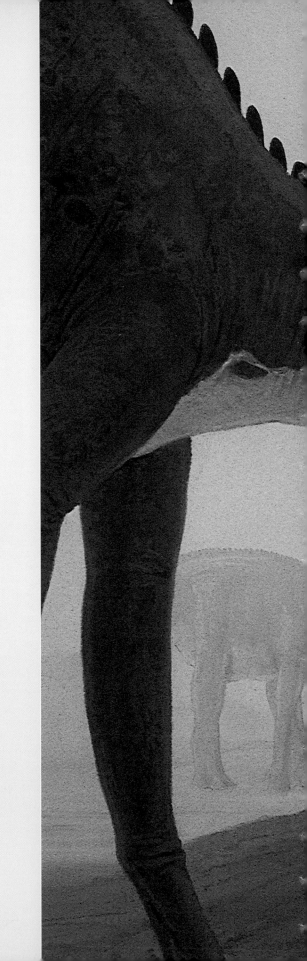

The drama of the disasters that created the ancient bone bed shouldn't overshadow what it represents—an enormous herd of dinosaurs. The part of the bone bed that Hooker studied in detail had fossils of animals from 13 feet (3.9 meters) all the way up to 24 feet (7.3 meters) long. Pits at the edges of the find, however, reveal bones from animals as small as 9 feet (2.74 meters) long. A 9-foot maiasaur was probably about a year old. At 24 feet, a maiasaur was fully grown. Why were thousands of maiasaurs, from yearlings to adults in age, together in one place at one time?

The maiasaurs belonged to a group of dinosaurs known as hadrosaurs. These plant-eating animals all had flattened snouts, shaped like a duck's bill. ➤

What Were the Maiasaurs?

Before we can understand the maiasaurs, we need to learn more about how they are related to other animals. Like all dinosaurs, maiasaurs were reptiles. While the dinosaurs most familiar to people are gigantic plant eaters such as *Apatosaurus* and large meat eaters such as *Tyrannosaurus,* the most common dinosaurs were probably the hadrosaurs, such as *Maiasaura.*

Hadrosaurs were plant eaters, with flattened snouts, like a duck's bill. For this reason, they are also called duckbills. At the end of their ducklike beak, hadrosaurs probably had horny lips attached to the bones. Ducks have such lips and use them to pluck off pieces of plants for food. Hadrosaurs appeared during the Cretaceous period in earth's history, which lasted from 142 million to 65.4 million years ago. The earliest hadrosaur fossils in North America are about 100 million years old.

There were two groups of hadrosaurs. One type, called crested hadrosaurs, had bony crests on the skull. The other group lacked crests and are called flat-headed hadrosaurs. *Maiasaura* was in the flat-headed group. The front of the hadrosaurs' snouts, used to pluck off leaves and other plant parts, had no teeth. But inside their mouths, they had rows of as many as two thousand small, crushing teeth for chewing their food. As the teeth wore down, new ones grew in to take their place. While many reptiles have teeth that can bite and slash, duckbills were among the few reptiles that could actually chew.

Duckbills lived along the coastal plains of Asia, Europe, and North and South America. They walked mainly on their hind legs but may have used their front legs when they stood still or walked slowly. Some hadrosaurs may have spent time in the water, collecting water plants for food. Others, such as *Maiasaura,* probably lived completely on land.

An artist's idea of how a crested hadrosaur named Corythosaurus *might have looked in life* ➤

Maiasaura *was a flat-headed hadrosaur.*

Life in Cretaceous Times

The geography of North America was very different in Cretaceous times than it is today. A giant inland sea, called the Western Interior Seaway, extended all the way from what is now the Gulf of Mexico up through North America to the Arctic Ocean. During the Cretaceous period, most of Mexico, what are now the coastal parts of the southern

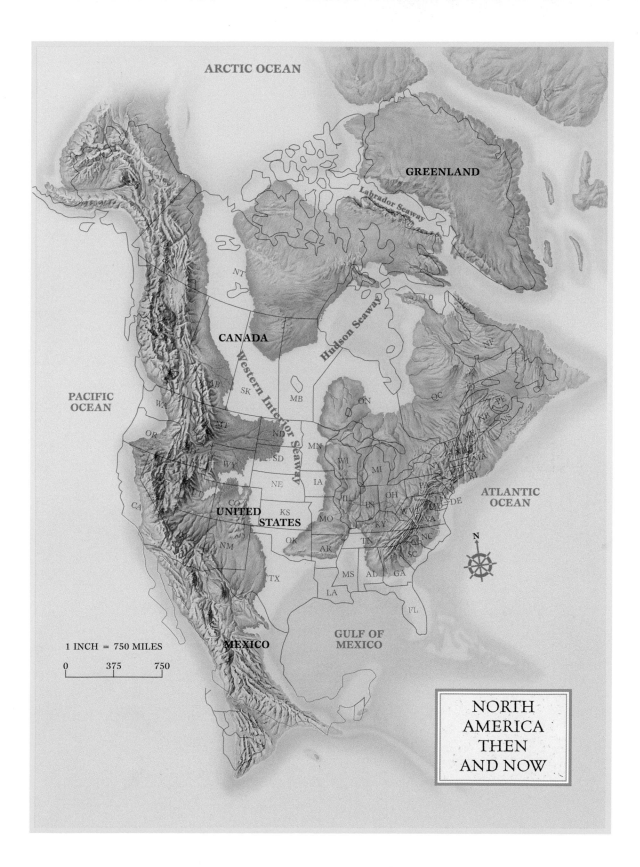

ARCTIC OCEAN

GREENLAND

Labrador Seaway

NT

Hudson Seaway

CANADA

PACIFIC
OCEAN

Western Interior Seaway

AB

SK

MB

ON

QC

NF

WA

MT

ND

MN

PE
AB
NS

OR

SD

WY

WI

MI

NY

ME

MA
RI

NE

IA

ATLANTIC
OCEAN

CA

IL

IN

OH

PA

CO

UNITED

STATES

KS

MO

KY

WV

MD DE
VA

NM

OK

AR

TN

NC

SC

N

TX

MS

AL

GA

LA

FL

1 INCH = 750 MILES

0   375   750

MEXICO

GULF OF
MEXICO

NORTH
AMERICA
THEN
AND NOW

Animals such as prehistoric birds and crocodiles lived at the same time as dinosaurs.

United States, the entire state of Florida, and parts of Central America were all underwater. At that time, the Rocky Mountains were forming, as volcanoes spewed forth rock and ash. The upper parts of the plains that lay between the developing mountains and the shores of the seaway were the home of *Maiasaura.*

Many other animals shared the land with the maiasaurs. Other dinosaurs, such as the meat eaters *Troodon* and *Albertosaurus* and plant eaters such as the horned dinosaur *Einiosaurus,* also lived

between the mountains and the sea. Amphibians and reptiles such as crocodiles and turtles lived along lakeshores. Many tiny mammals lived on the land. Flying reptiles called pterosaurs, early sorts of birds, and winged insects such as dragonflies ruled the skies.

Plants were abundant and varied back then. Most trees were evergreens. Magnolia-like trees and flowering dogwood-like trees also dotted the forests. Ferns and palms were also common, as were large palm-like plants called cycads. There was no such thing yet as grass. Instead, ferns and low leafy plants covered the plains.

Dinosaurs of the Ages

The dinosaurs lived during a time in earth's history that scientists call the Mesozoic era. The Mesozoic era is separated into three divisions, called periods. First came the Triassic period (245 million to 208 million years ago), then the Jurassic (208 million to 142 million years ago), and finally the Cretaceous (142 million to 65.4 million years ago). The first dinosaurs appeared late in the Triassic, when all the land on earth was one big continent. They evolved from meat-eating reptiles called thecodonts. Unlike other early reptiles, some thecodonts walked on their hind legs instead of getting about on all fours. The first dinosaurs lived much like their thecodont ancestors, except they were probably faster, more efficient hunters.

During the Triassic period, the dinosaurs evolved into two separate groups. The group called the Saurischia, which means "lizard-hipped," came first, about 225 million years ago. In a saurischian dinosaur, the hipbone, called the pubic bone, projects forward, like that of its ancestors. Also like their ancestors, the early saurischians were fast-moving hunters.

Soon after the Saurischia appeared, the first bird-hipped (Ornithischia) dinosaurs showed up. Bird-hipped dinosaurs evolved either from the Saurischia or, less likely, from an ancestor similar to the ancestor of the Saurischia. In ornithischian dinosaurs, the pubic bone points backward, like that of modern birds. The Ornithischia were all plant eaters and included some of the most familiar dinosaurs—*Stegosaurus*, with impressive bony plates along its back; the large, armored dinosaurs such as the ankylosaurs, some with clubs on the ends of their tails; and *Triceratops*, the 24-foot (7.3-meter) rhinoceros-like creature with its

impressive horns and wide neck shield. The duck-billed dinosaurs, such as *Maiasaura*, are also ornithischians.

While the bird-hipped dinosaurs were evolving into a vast array of plant eaters, the saurischians split into two types—meat eaters and plant eaters. During the Jurassic period, such familiar lizard-hipped plant eaters as *Diplodocus*, with its long neck and tail, appeared, as well as hunters such as *Allosaurus*, which may have hunted in packs. Although the film *Jurassic Park* featured a very frightening *Tyrannosaurus rex*, this gigantic meat eater didn't appear until the Cretaceous period, well after the Jurassic period had ended.

One of the great mysteries of science is the disappearance of the dinosaurs. Why did these incredibly successful creatures, which survived through so many changes on the planet, die out at the end of the Cretaceous period? Many scientists blame an asteroid that struck the earth 65 million years ago, sending up huge amounts of dust, blocking the sun, which nourishes plant life. As plants died off, so would the dinosaurs that fed on them, followed by the meat eaters, which depended on the plant eaters.

Many paleontologists today believe that birds are descended from dinosaurs. If true, dinosaurs did not become extinct—they still live among us. Strangely enough, birds would have evolved from saurischians, developing their birdlike hips later.

Many artists have devoted their professional lives to illustrating dinosaurs and their prehistoric world. This great mural, which took more than three years to paint, is by Rudolph Zallinger and hangs in the Peabody Museum at Yale University. Many familiar dinosaurs are illustrated, including Tyrannosaurus, Apatosaurus, *and* Stegosaurus. *The mural also shows other prehistoric animals such as pterosaurs, crocodilians, and a dragonfly, along with prehistoric plants.*

4

JACK HORNER AND DINOSAURS

All his life, Jack Horner has been interested
in dinosaurs. He studied biology, geology, and
paleontology at the University of Montana,
but he never finished his college education.
In 1975, he got a job as a fossil preparator at
Princeton University in New Jersey.
Preparators often spend their lives piecing
together bits of fossils discovered by
paleontologists during their seasons in the
field. But Horner was lucky. His boss, Don
Baird, encouraged Horner to do his own
research. So every summer, Horner would
head out to Montana and to Alberta, Canada,
looking for dinosaurs.

*Jack Horner studies the ground carefully, looking
for fossils.* ➤

Rediscovering Forgotten Fossils

Over the years, Horner kept finding duckbill fossils, so his interest in these dinosaurs increased. Then, in 1978, Baird and Horner found some fossils hidden away in the collection at Princeton University. They had been collected around 1900 in Montana. When Horner looked at these fossils closely, he discovered that many of them belonged to juvenile duckbills.

Back then, fossils of young dinosaurs were very rare, and scientists puzzled over why so few had been found. The most likely explanation had to do with how fossils form. The dinosaurs whose fossils have been discovered lived mostly along low coastal plains, where conditions, such as periodic flooding, favored the formation of fossils. On higher ground, where slopes are steeper, fossilization rarely occurs. So if these dinosaurs moved to higher ground to lay eggs and raise young, few fossils of eggs and young would be found.

Horner was excited by the discovery of the juvenile fossils, whatever the reason for their rarity. He realized that if he went to Montana and looked for fossils himself, he had a good chance of finding some rare ones that could shed light on how dinosaurs lived.

Horner's Finds

Through a series of lucky coincidences, Horner and his friend and fellow dinosaur hunter Bob Makela ended up in the rock shop owned by Marion and John Brandvold in the tiny town of Bynum, Montana, in July 1978. The Brandvolds had found some puzzling dinosaur fossils, and Horner and Makela hoped they could help identify them. When Mrs. Brandvold brought out the bones, Horner knew immediately that they belonged to duckbills. One was a piece of rib; the other was the upper part of a thighbone. But they were miniatures. If whole, the thighbone would have been only a few inches in length. The thighbone of an adult duckbill would be many times longer, about 4 feet (1.2 meters) long. These were clearly the bones of babies.

Mrs. Brandvold had more fossil bones. When the men told her

Collecting and Preparing Fossils

Paleontologists know where to look for fossils. They usually find specimens by carefully looking over promising ground to see what the wearing of wind and weather has revealed. After finding a bit of bone showing at the surface, the team gently removes overlying rock in the area until the fossil layer is revealed. Sometimes they divide the site into grids and map out and label which fossils lie where within the grid lines. The dirt around the fossils is gently removed using an ice pick and a toothbrush, then brushed away with a whisk broom. As it is uncovered, each bit of fossil surface is coated with a liquid plastic called polyvinyl acetate to strengthen it.

The work is time-consuming and requires plenty of patience—nudge loose some rock, brush the dirt away, paint the newly exposed surface. Eventually, there lies a fossil attached to the rock only on the underside. That's when the fossil is encased in plaster of Paris and burlap to hold it firmly together. Then the casted fossil is broken free from the rock.

Over the digging season, large numbers of fossils build up, all safely protected in their plaster casts. During the winter in the laboratory, the casts are removed and the fossils are cleaned, identified, and varnished for protection.

Paleontology is mostly hard, patient work, carefully scratching away dirt and rock to reveal fossils.

what they were, she gave them the fossils. Then she and her husband took Horner and Makela to the place where the fossils had been found. The spot was just a bump in the landscape, a knob of stone eroded from ancient mud that stood up only about 4 feet (1.2 meters) from the surrounding landscape. But that small lump turned out to be one of the most important paleontological finds of the century.

A Nest of Duckbills

It didn't take Horner and Makela long to realize that the modest mudstone knob was actually the preserved nest of a dinosaur. Only once before, in 1922, had paleontologists found dinosaur nests. That find had been in the Gobi Desert of Mongolia, and was one of the most

A nest of baby maiasaur skeletons. These models were carefully designed by scientists.

exciting events in paleontology. The Gobi discovery consisted of four nests containing eggs. Now, fifty-six years later, another nest had been discovered. And instead of eggs, it contained the remains of fifteen young dinosaurs, each about 3 feet (.9 meter) long.

The outside of the knob was made up of red mudstone, while the inside, where the bones of baby dinosaurs lay jumbled together with bits of broken eggshell, consisted of green mudstone. Millions of years ago, a mother dinosaur had made a nest, forming a mound of dirt with a 6-foot (1.8-meter) wide bowl-shaped depression in the center. There she had laid her eggs. The baby dinosaurs had stayed in the nest, growing in size, until some disaster struck that killed them all when they were about 3 feet (.9 meter) long. Their bodies lay in the nest and rotted, leaving their bones.

The bones would have disappeared, too, if a nearby stream hadn't flooded, depositing mud in the nest and burying the bones. Then, bit by bit, the bones became fossils as minerals in the groundwater filled in parts of the bone that had contained living tissue. In the process, even the minute microscopic structure of the bones was preserved.

Horner could tell by examining the form of the bones that they came from young dinosaurs. The vertebrae, for example, weren't fused as they were in adults, and the ends of the long bones weren't completely developed. He knew the dinosaurs weren't hatchlings— their teeth were worn down, indicating they'd been feeding for quite a while.

5

THE "GOOD MOTHER LIZARDS"

Ever since the first sensational discovery of a nest of baby dinosaurs, Jack Horner has been studying these fascinating ancient creatures. Now he is officially Dr. Horner, with a degree awarded by the University of Montana, where he had gone to college. He is curator of paleontology at the Museum of the Rockies in Bozeman, Montana. (A curator oversees the care of a collection.) He was an adviser on the films *Jurassic Park* and *The Lost World: Jurassic Park.* His discoveries and theories about how dinosaurs lived have helped change how people today think about them.

This model of a mother maiasaur with her nest of hatching eggs is in the Natural History Museum in London, England. ➤

Extinct But Successful

Even today, some people think of dinosaurs as an unsuccessful biological experiment. After all, they have disappeared from the planet—unless, as some scientists believe, birds evolved from dinosaurs. When we describe something that is out-of-date, we often call it a "dinosaur." But dinosaurs evolved and thrived over a period of about 140 million years. Primates, the group to which monkeys, apes, and humans belong, came into being only about the time dinosaurs disappeared, 65 million years ago. Our species has only been around for a few hundred thousand years.

Many scientists consider the dinosaurs to be the most successful animals with backbones yet to inhabit the earth. Hundreds and hundreds of different dinosaur species evolved. Some were smaller than a chicken, and others were the largest land animals that ever lived. Dinosaurs ate all sorts of food and thrived in all kinds of land habitats.

Dinosaurs were once depicted as slow and stupid. But we now know that many of them showed complex behavior and high intelligence, and some may have run faster than a horse. Some small hunting dinosaurs were probably as intelligent as birds are today.

More about Maiasaura

Horner first described *Maiasaura* on the basis of the adult dinosaur skull discovered near the first nest he found. A skull can tell a scientist a great deal about how an animal lived and is one of the easier ways of telling species apart. Most North American hadrosaur skulls have larger openings for the nostrils and shorter snouts than *Maiasaura*. Although *Maiasaura* belongs to the flat-headed hadrosaurs, it still had a tiny crest on its skull. In life, this crest was probably topped by decorative skin that could have been important for social or mating behavior.

The biggest maiasaurs were about 30 feet (9 meters) long from nose to tip of the tail. Scientists estimate that such an animal would have weighed about three tons, the weight of a small female elephant.

An adult maiasaur skull

An average adult was around 25 feet (7.6 meters) long. Maiasaurs were rather slender in build, not stocky like elephants.

Nesting in Colonies

Every summer, Horner and his crew headed north from Bozeman, Montana, to dig and study, every year making new and important discoveries. In addition to finding nests and eggs from other species, they uncovered a total of eight maiasaur nests in one area. The nests were spaced about 23 feet (7 meters) apart—approximately the same length as an adult maiasaur—and seemed to be part of a larger nesting area. Two of the nests, including the one mentioned earlier, contained the

Are Birds Living Dinosaurs?

Many paleontologists like to say that the dinosaurs didn't become extinct—they are alive today, living among us as birds. We've known for a long time that birds evolved from reptiles of some kind. But whether or not those reptiles were dinosaurs is not known for sure.

The question of bird evolution hinges on the structure of the skeletons of birds and those of extinct reptiles. Those who say birds originated from dinosaurs point to the skeleton of a very early bird, *Archeopteryx*. Some fossils of *Archeopteryx* have not just the skeleton but also the impressions of feathers in the rock. These feathers are already much like those of modern birds. But unlike birds, *Archeopteryx* had a long, bony tail and a beak with teeth.

The skeleton of *Archeopteryx* is very similar to that of small theropod dinosaurs. The theropods were lizard-hipped dinosaurs that ran about on their hind legs (*Tyrannosaurus rex* was a theropod). They were active hunters and may have been quite intelligent. The skeletons of these animals and *Archeopteryx* are so much alike that one featherless *Archeopteryx* fossil was misidentified as a theropod called *Compsognathus*. Altogether, scientists can list two hundred features of anatomy shared by birds and dinosaurs.

Evidence for the theory that birds evolved from dinosaurs comes from various fossils. In 1996, for example, Argentinian paleontologists found fossils of a new dinosaur species. This theropod, which they named *Unenlagia camahuensis*, had a large body and small arms that could be folded like the wings of a bird. Its shoulder joint would also have enabled *Unenlagia* to raise its arms the way a bird strokes its wings while flying. Its arms were too small to function as wings, but this interesting creature could have spread out its arms for balance while running. There's one big problem with *Unenlagia*, however—it lived almost 60 million years after *Archeopteryx*. Supporters of dinosaur origins for birds aren't bothered by this fact. They say that *Unenlagia* was a "living fossil," an animal very much like its ancestors that survived with little change for millions of years, as have alligators and sharks today.

In 1997, some scientists once again challenged the idea that birds evolved from dinosaurs. They examined the finger bones of some birds and theropod dinosaurs closely and claimed that they are not as similar as other scientists think they are.

Perhaps soon we will have more evidence about the origin of birds. A very exciting new site in China contains fossils never seen before. Paleontologists who have visited this site say that it represents the

A fossilized Archeopteryx *skeleton*

period from about 140 million to 120 million years ago. Among its many fossils are those of early birds, which could tell us more about where birds came from, as well as a possible feathered dinosaur.

But meanwhile, it is interesting to think that the dinosaurs are still with us, flying through our neighborhoods every day. Whether or not birds evolved from dinosaurs, the behavior of modern birds has provided useful models for dinosaur behavior, such as nesting in colonies, migration, and parental care of the young.

fossil bones of young maiasaurs. The babies in the second nest were only 14 inches (36 centimeters) long.

Horner and his coworkers also found other *Maiasaura* nesting grounds with baby dinosaurs in them. The scientists never uncovered bones of young smaller than 14 inches (36 centimeters), probably the size at hatching, or larger than 3½ feet (1 meter) long, the size at which the youngsters probably left the nest. They also found remains of some unhatched eggs, with fossilized embryos inside. But except for the nests with unhatched eggs, the *Maiasaura* nests consistently contained crushed pieces of shell, indicating that the baby dinosaurs had trampled them while remaining in the nest. In the nests of another dinosaur species, complete pieces of fossilized hatched eggs were found. The young of that species must have left their nests immediately after hatching, as do baby crocodilians (crocodiles, alligators, and their relatives) today.

Fossilized Maiasaura *eggs*

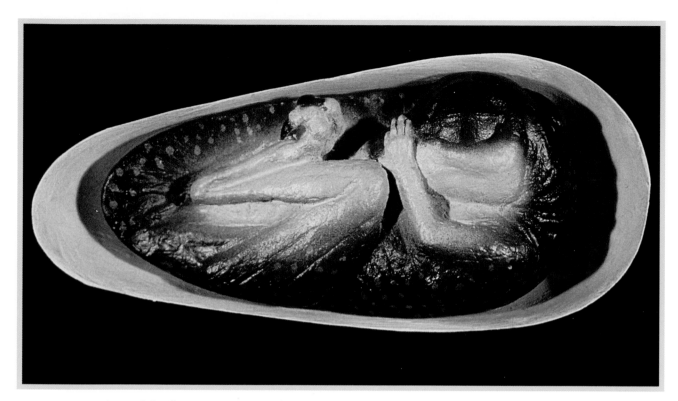

A model of a maiasaur embryo inside the egg

Caring for the Young

Why did the maiasaur young stay in their nests? It's possible that the babies left the nest to feed and returned to rest. But that sort of behavior isn't known among animals that live today. Only when one or both parents care for the young, gathering food and bringing it back to the nest, do animal young remain there. Horner believes this is the only reasonable explanation for finding babies in the nest—one or both parents brought them food there, instead of laying the eggs and leaving the young to survive on their own, as do most reptiles today. Maiasaurs, he claims, are more like birds than reptiles in their behavior. It's a revolutionary idea, one that Horner honored in his naming of this new kind of dinosaur—*Maiasaura* means "good mother lizard" in Greek.

Certainly, there are similarities between maiasaurs and modern birds. Many birds nest in colonies, with their nests spaced about the

same distance apart as the size of an adult bird, just like the maiasaur nests. The birds sit on the nest, keeping the eggs warm, and feed the young after hatching.

Maiasaurs almost certainly didn't incubate their eggs—the animals were too large. The eggs were most likely covered with plant material, which rotted, creating warmth for the eggs. Crocodilians and some birds use plants in this way today. Perhaps, like many crocodilians, the female maiasaur stayed near her nest, protecting the eggs from predators. No reptiles living today feed their young in the nest after hatching, but some mother crocodilians do stay nearby and defend their young.

◄ *This model of a mother maiasaur with her young is in the Museum of the Rockies in Bozeman, Montana.*

6

PUTTING IT TOGETHER

Before the 1970s, most of what we knew about dinosaurs was about their bones, not their lives. Paleontologists could figure out from their teeth what sort of food dinosaurs ate. They could tell what sort of habitat they occupied from the plants found with them. But few paleontologists concerned themselves with dinosaur ecology. Now, thanks to Horner and other scientists who piece together the evidence they find like detectives trying to solve a crime, we have ideas about how some dinosaurs, such as *Maiasaura*, might have lived. Much of what is presented is still largely theory, not proven fact. But it gives us a window on what the world might have been like so long ago.

◄ *This painting of a maiasaur nesting site was based on the evidence found by Jack Horner and his colleagues.*

49

New Lives Begin

When it came time to lay their eggs, adult female maiasaurs dug out their nests, making bowl-shaped depressions into which they each laid about twenty eggs. They probably covered the eggs with plant material. As the vegetation rotted, it would have helped keep the eggs warm so the embryos inside could develop.

When the young were ready to hatch, they might have started making peeping noises, as young alligators do today. The mother maiasaur, upon hearing the peeping, might have done what the alligator does—help crack the shells of some of the eggs if the young are having trouble breaking out.

Once the young were hatched, the mother would have searched for food, gathering plants for her babies and dropping them into the nest. Her youngsters could concentrate all their energy on growing fast, since they didn't use energy moving about, searching for something to eat. They probably grew from their hatching size—about 14 inches (.3 meter)—to 3½ feet (1 meter) long in about five months.

Growing Up

Since the largest young found in nests were about 3 feet (.9 meter) long, Horner thinks they left the nest at about this size. What happened to them next is a mystery. No fossils of young maiasaurs between 3½ and 9 feet (1 and 2.74 meters) in length have been found as yet. Horner suggests that they stayed with their mothers, each family living on its own, for a year or so. These dinosaur families, he thinks, lived in forested valleys close to the mountains, in the kind of environment that rarely forms fossils.

Then, he believes, when the young dinosaurs were old enough to take care of themselves, the families joined up into large herds, like the one whose bones he and his associates found. As we have seen, these herds consisted of thousands of animals ranging in size from about 9 feet (2.74 meters) long to full-grown adults. Many large grass-eating mammals of today, such as wildebeests in Africa, migrate in

Maiasaur hatchlings break free from their eggs in this model nest.

The reconstructed skeleton of a maiasaur in the process of hatching

herds of countless thousands. Before Europeans came to North America, bison traveled over the prairies in unimaginably gigantic herds. Maiasaurs had no grass to eat, but bushes probably covered the plains then the way grasses do today.

Maiasaurs may have lived in herds and roamed the plains, feeding on bushes.

Some scientists have doubts that the fossils found by Horner's group really do represent one large maiasaur herd. The estimate of the size of the herd, at least ten thousand individuals, may not be accurate. It is based on the idea that each of the sites the group studied is part of a large bone bed that extends relatively evenly over the area between the sites. Only by uncovering the whole area could we be certain this is true. Horner's critics also object to comparing dinosaur herds with the giant mammal herds of today. The grass on which animals like wildebeests and bison feed grows fast. The kinds of plants maiasaurs ate probably grew much more slowly. The critics think that such slow-growing plants wouldn't have provided enough food to feed such large groups of dinosaurs.

Horner believes that when the breeding season arrived, the adult maiasaurs traveled to the nesting grounds to begin new families. After two or three years, the young maiasaurs were old enough themselves to breed. Then they would have joined their elders and begun the cycle of life once more.

Changing Ideas

The revolution in how we view dinosaurs began more than twenty-five years ago. Back then, we knew much less not only about dinosaurs but also about the reptiles that live today. Most scientists then didn't believe that crocodilians take care of their young after hatching—people thought reptiles weren't intelligent enough for such behavior. We also didn't understand that the terms *warm-blooded* and *cold-blooded* are not absolutes—some animals have a partial ability to control their body temperature.

Science continues to bring new ideas about how living things function, both in the present and in the past. It's important to keep an open mind, because our increasing knowledge can change what we consider to be "facts." For example, Horner and his colleagues recently discovered that at least one dinosaur, *Troodon formosus,* actually incubated its eggs. But this information came at the expense of another idea—that *Troodon* was a predator that ate the eggs of another dinosaur. The skeleton of an adult *Troodon* had been found atop a nest thought to be of the dinosaur *Orodromeus.* But after further finds and closer study, the scientists now realize that the *Troodon* specimen

Were Dinosaurs Warm-Blooded?

Paleontologists who study dinosaurs disagree about an exciting idea that was first suggested in the late 1960s. Before then, dinosaurs had been thought of by most people as slow, cold-blooded creatures, similar to some modern reptiles. But as scientists learned more and more about the skeletons and bone structure of dinosaurs, they began to see that the old idea just didn't fit. Could dinosaurs have been warm-blooded?

For one thing, dinosaurs stood differently than reptiles such as lizards. A lizard's legs go out to the sides. When a lizard runs, it has to lift its body from the ground as it scampers off. Then it rests again with its belly to the ground. It doesn't take much energy for the lizard to lie there with the ground supporting its weight. Dinosaurs, on the other hand, carried their legs underneath their bodies. They couldn't plop themselves down on their bellies to rest. Holding up the entire body most of the time would take a lot of energy.

Like dinosaurs, birds and mammals hold their legs under their bodies. So how are birds and mammals different from lizards? How do they get the energy they need to stay upright and active? Most birds and mammals are warm-blooded. Warm-blooded animals have a high metabolic rate. They keep a relatively constant body temperature that is warmer than the outside air. This allows them to be physically active even when it's cold outside.

Most of the reptiles and fish alive today, however, are what is popularly called cold-blooded. This doesn't mean their blood is cold. It means their body temperature is affected by the temperature of their surroundings. If a lizard sits in the sun, it soaks up heat, and its body becomes warm. This allows the lizard to skitter away if danger threatens. After a cold night, a lizard is sluggish. Its body is cool, and it can't move quickly.

So what about dinosaurs? Some paleontologists argue that dinosaurs must have been warm-blooded, since they were so active. What sort of evidence is there, beyond the way dinosaurs walked, to suggest that they were warm-blooded? One clue may lie in the structure of their bones. The bones of birds and mammals contain many blood vessels, which carry nutrients and energy. Reptiles, on the other hand, have fewer blood vessels in their bones. Dinosaur bones often look more like the bones of birds and mammals than like those of reptiles.

Other scientists think there isn't enough evidence to prove that dinosaurs were warm-blooded. They point out, for example, that many dinosaurs were so huge they would hold the heat from their metabolism deep within their bodies. They would stay warm without having to generate extra heat the way birds and mammals do.

Chances are no one will ever be able to prove that dinosaurs were or were not warm-blooded. There were so many different kinds of dinosaurs living over a period of so many millions of years that it is possible some were cold-blooded and others were warm-blooded, depending on their size, habitat, and lifestyle. Or, as many paleontologists believe, they could lie somewhere between the two extremes.

wasn't feeding on *Orodromeus* eggs—it was incubating its own!

What new information might the future bring about *Maiasaura?* Horner's group is just starting a new study of the giant bone bed to see what more they can learn. The scientists suspect the bed may be much larger than they thought. Who knows how many dinosaurs might have been in that herd, perhaps a hundred thousand instead of ten thousand? Maybe one day we'll know, and maybe we won't.

Maiasaura *in Time*

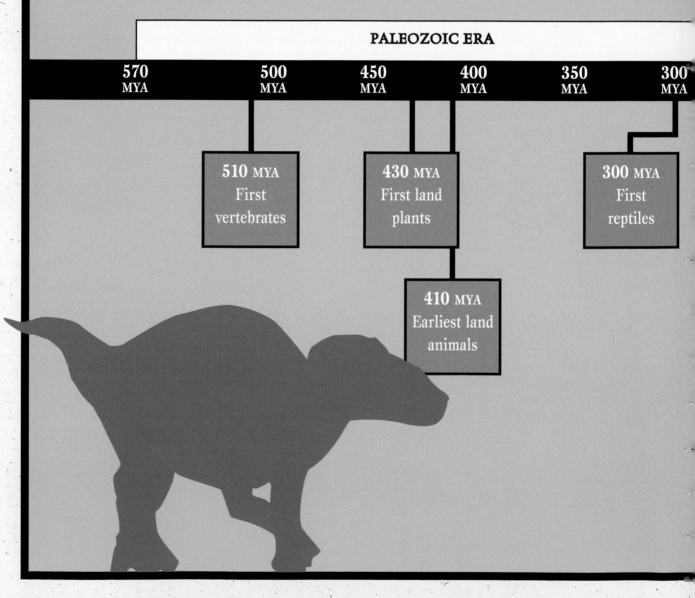

PALEOZOIC ERA

| 570 MYA | 500 MYA | 450 MYA | 400 MYA | 350 MYA | 300 MYA |

510 MYA
First vertebrates

430 MYA
First land plants

300 MYA
First reptiles

410 MYA
Earliest land animals

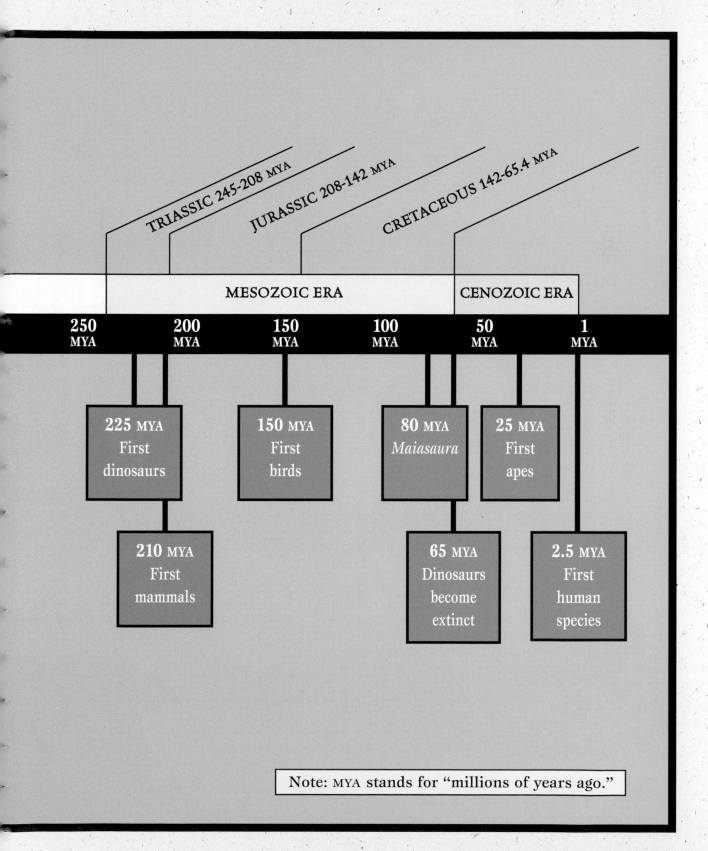

TRIASSIC 245-208 MYA

JURASSIC 208-142 MYA

CRETACEOUS 142-65.4 MYA

MESOZOIC ERA   CENOZOIC ERA

250 MYA   200 MYA   150 MYA   100 MYA   50 MYA   1 MYA

225 MYA
First
dinosaurs

150 MYA
First
birds

80 MYA
Maiasaura

25 MYA
First
apes

210 MYA
First
mammals

65 MYA
Dinosaurs
become
extinct

2.5 MYA
First
human
species

Note: MYA stands for "millions of years ago."

Glossary

bird-hipped dinosaur: A dinosaur belonging to the group Ornithischia, with the bones of the pelvis arranged somewhat like that of birds.

cold-blooded animal: An animal such as a lizard whose body temperature varies depending on its environment.

Cretaceous: The last period of the Mesozoic era, about 142 million to 65.4 million years ago.

crocodilian: A reptile belonging to the crocodile family, which includes twenty-two species of crocodiles, alligators, caimans, and others.

curator: The person who oversees the care of a collection, especially in a museum.

duck-billed dinosaur: A dinosaur belonging to the hadrosaurs, which all had a ducklike bill at the front of their mouths.

Einiosaurus: A horned dinosaur that shared the land with maiasaurs.

fossil: The preserved remains or traces of living things of the past.

fossilization: The processes by which fossils form.

geology: The study of rocks and minerals.

hadrosaur: Another name for a duck-billed dinosaur.

Jurassic: The middle period of the Mesozoic era, about 208 million to 142 million years ago.

lizard-hipped dinosaur: A dinosaur belonging to the group Saurischia, with the bones of the pelvis arranged in a way similar to that of modern reptiles.

maiasaur: A dinosaur belonging to the scientific genus *Maiasaura.* So far, scientists have only described one species, *Maiasaura peeblesorum.*

metabolic rate: The amount of energy an animal uses up during a specific period of time. An animal with a high metabolic rate uses more energy than one with a low metabolic rate.

Ornithischia: The scientific name for the bird-hipped dinosaurs.

Orodromeus: A small bird-hipped dinosaur that lived at the same time and place as *Maiasaura.*

paleontologist: A scientist who studies fossils to learn about living things of the past.

polyvinyl acetate: A plastic that paleontologists use to coat fossils in the field to strengthen them.

Saurischia: The scientific name for the lizard-hipped dinosaurs.

sedimentary rock: Rock that forms when layers of mud or sand build up; the layers weigh down on one another, gradually hardening into rock.

site: The place where something is found or located.

species: A specific kind of living thing, usually defined as the populations of organisms that can breed together naturally.

thecodonts: The reptiles that were the ancestors of dinosaurs and crocodilians.

theropods: Meat-eating dinosaurs that ran on two legs and may have included the ancestor of birds.

Triassic: The first period of the Mesozoic era, about 245 million to 208 million years ago.

Troodon: A small meat-eating dinosaur recently found to have incubated its eggs.

warm-blooded animal: An animal that can keep its body at a constant temperature regardless of outside temperature.

Western Interior Seaway: A body of water that extended through the center of North America, all the way from the Gulf of Mexico to the Arctic Ocean, during the Cretaceous period.

For Further Reading

Gore, Rick. "Dinosaurs." *National Geographic,* January 1993, pp. 2–54.

Horner, John R. "The Nesting Behavior of Dinosaurs." *Scientific American,* April 1984, pp. 130–137.

Horner, John R., and Edwin Dobb. *Dinosaur Lives.* New York: HarperCollins, 1997.

Horner, John R., and James Gorman. *Digging Dinosaurs.* New York: HarperCollins, 1988.

Bibliography

Coombs, Walter P., Jr. "Modern Analogs for Dinosaur Nesting and Parental Behavior." In *Paleobiology of the Dinosaurs,* edited by James O. Farlow. Boulder, CO: Geological Society of America, 1989.

Gore, Rick. "Dinosaurs." *National Geographic,* January 1993, pp. 2–54.

Horner, John R. "Evidence of Colonial Nesting and 'Site Fidelity' among Ornithischian Dinosaurs." *Nature,* Vol. 297: pp. 675–676, 1982.

———. "The Nesting Behavior of Dinosaurs." *Scientific American,* April 1984, pp. 130–137.

Horner, John R., and Edwin Dobb. *Dinosaur Lives.* New York: HarperCollins, 1997.

Horner, John R., and James Gorman. *Digging Dinosaurs.* New York: HarperCollins, 1988.

Horner, John R., and R. Makela. "Nest of Juveniles Provides Evidence of Family Structure among Dinosaurs." *Nature,* Vol. 282: pp. 296–298, 1979.

Horner, John R., and David B. Weishampel. "A Comparative Embryological Study of Two Ornithischian Dinosaurs." *Nature,* Vol. 332: pp. 256–258, 1988.

Lambert, David, and the Diagram Group. *The Field Guide to Prehistoric Life.* New York: Facts On File, 1985.

Monostersky, Richard. "A Fowl Fight: Fossil Finds Recharge Debate about Birds and Dinosaurs." *Science News,* Vol. 152: pp. 120–121, 1997.

Scarre, Chris. *Smithsonian Timelines of the Ancient World.* New York: Dorling Kindersley, 1993.

Science News, May 3, 1997, p. 271.

Simpson, George Gaylord. *Life of the Past: An Introduction to Paleontology.* New Haven: Yale University Press, 1953.

Varricchio, David J., Frankie Jackson, John J. Borkowski, and John R. Horner. "Nest and Egg Clutches of the Dinosaur *Troodon formosus* and the Evolution of Avian Reproductive Traits." *Nature,* Vol. 385: pp. 247–250, 1997.

Weishampel, David B., Peter Dodson, and Halszka Osmólska. *The Dinosauria.* Berkeley: University of California Press, 1990.

Index

Page numbers for illustrations are in boldface

Jurassic period, 30, 31, 57

lizards, 54
Lost World: Jurassic Park, The (film), 38

maiasaurs, **18–19**, **22–23**, 24, **26**, **38–39**, 40–41, **41**, **52**
  baby, 36–37, **36**, 50, **51**
  caring for the young, 45–47, **46**
  duck-billed dinosaurs, 22, 36–37, **36**
  during Cretaceous period, 28–29
  eggs, **44–45**
  giant maiasaur bone bed, 6, **7–9**, **14–15**, 22
  Maiasaura peeblesorum, 12
  Maiasaura skeletons, **12**, **36**
  Maiasaura in time, 56–57
  nesting grounds, 41, 44, **48–49**
  young, 50, 52–53
Makela, Bob, 34, 36
mammals, 52–53, 54
meat-eating dinosaurs, 24, 28–29
Mesozoic era, 30, 57
Montana, 6, 17, 32, 34, 41, 47
mudslides, 16, 17
Museum of the Rockies, 6, 38, 47

nests and eggs, dinosaur, 21, 36–37, **36**, **38–39**, 41, 44, **44**, **45**, **46**, **48–49**, **51**
Nose Cone site, 11, 13

ornithischian dinosaurs, 30–31
Orodromeus, 53, 55

paleontologists, 6, 10, 13, 14, 21, 31, **35**, 42–43, 54
Paleozoic era, 56–57
plant-eating dinosaurs, **22–23**, 28–29
plants, prehistoric, 29, **30–31**, 53
primates, 40
pterosaurs, 29, **30–31**

reptiles, 24, 54

saurischian dinosaurs, 30
sedimentary rocks, 21
shale, 21
Stegosaurus, 30, **30–31**

thecodonts, 30
theropods, 42
Triassic period, 30, 57
Triceratops, 30–31
Troodon, 28–29, 53, 55
turtles, 29
Tyrannosaurus rex, 24, **30–31**, 31, 42

Unenlagia camahuensis, 42

volcanoes, 17, 21
  volcanic ash, 14, 16, **18–19**

warm-blooded animals, 53, 54

About the Author

Dorothy Patent is the author of more than one hundred science and nature books for children and has won numerous awards for her writing. She has a Ph.D. in zoology from the University of California, Berkeley.

Although trained as a biologist, Dorothy has always been fascinated by the human past. At home, next to the books about animals, her shelves are jammed with titles such as *Mysteries of the Past.* When the opportunity came to write about other times and cultures for children, Dorothy plunged enthusiastically into the project. In the process of researching the FROZEN IN TIME series, she said, "I have had some great adventures and have come to understand much more deeply what it means to be human."

Dorothy lives in Missoula, Montana, with her husband, Greg, and their two dogs, Elsa and Ninja. They enjoy living close to nature in their home at the edge of a forest.